60 Minutes to
Reveal Your Purpose

Diane Gorsky

Published by New Generation Publishing in 2023

Copyright © Diane Gorsky 2023

First Edition

The author asserts the moral right under the Copyright, Designs and Patents Act 1988 to be identified as the author of this work.

All Rights reserved. No part of this publication may be reproduced, stored in a retrieval system or transmitted, in any form or by any means without the prior consent of the author, nor be otherwise circulated in any form of binding or cover other than that which it is published and without a similar condition being imposed on the subsequent purchaser.

ISBN   978-1-80369-703-1

www.newgeneration-publishing.com

New Generation Publishing

Dedication

Life purpose is an essential part of human wellbeing, with decades of research supporting its value. This booklet is dedicated to people who seek purpose but for whom the words remain elusive. This guide is for you. Your life has purpose, expressed through your unique nature and choices. If you aim to explore life purpose, there is support and guidance for you here.

Welcome to purpose

Are you by intrigued by the prospect of living with purpose? Or somewhat skeptical that purpose really matters? You may be rethinking your purpose or getting started for the first time. I welcome you to try the REVEAL approach, designed to be inviting and accessible. Purposeful living is a lifelong practice. It's hoped this engaging and interactive tool will support you along the way.

What is life purpose?

Purpose frames the meaning of your life. It guides your choices and provides direction. It's a feeling that your life is worthwhile. Finding life purpose, however, is not a simple task. Like many people, I struggled to put my personal purpose into words. In response, I developed REVEAL as a practical and original tool to support purpose exploration.

What's ahead?

- Introduction to life purpose, benefits and challenges
- Demystifying purpose
- The REVEAL tool, templates and instructions
- Guidance on living and enacting life purpose

History of purpose

What is my purpose? This fundamental question dates back to the philosophers of ancient Greece. The world's great thinkers reflected on the power of meaningful purpose that is unselfish, uplifting and altruistic. It's this type of purpose that provides focus, stability and fulfillment.

Purpose today

More recently, researchers have focused on purposeful living and its positive impact on the mind and body. Life purpose is associated with a remarkable range of benefits, from a subjective sense of happiness to lower stress levels. People with a clear sense of purpose experience increased resilience, physical and mental health, confidence and self-esteem. Purpose is also associated with motivation, commitment and engagement at work.

Purpose is difficult to articulate: part 1

While people may feel a general sense of purpose, articulating that purpose is often a challenge. Purpose is notoriously abstract and amorphous, and can be difficult to put into words. Our daily routines and busy schedules may further cloud our awareness. As a consequence, we may find ourselves off-track and unfulfilled. Without clarity of purpose, we cannot reap its many benefits.

Purpose is difficult to articulate: part 2

People generally seek purpose at times of transition, uncertainty, anxiety or self-doubt. However, cognitive psychology tells us that unsettling life changes and strong emotion inhibit the thinking process required to explore abstract ideas such as purpose. In other words, we are motivated to explore life meaning and purpose at the time when our mental processes are at their lowest ebb.

Purpose: myth 1

Myth 1: life purpose is expressed as a catchy slogan or passion. While this is a popular view, it fails to recognize humans as multifaceted. In reality, people have *purposes* with multiple dimensions and elements involved. Having several sources of meaning strengthens resilience. This broader perspective releases us from the daunting pressure of embracing a superhuman mission or aligning all actions behind a single, heroic cause.

Purpose: myth 2

Myth 2: purpose can only be discovered through deep contemplation. While introspection and meditation are time-honoured practices, these approaches do not work for everyone. After journaling and self-refection, you may still feel stuck and unable to bring purpose to the forefront. When words don't flow easily, open-ended contemplation may not be the most effective.

Breaking through "purpose block"

Much like writer's block, we can experience "purpose block" – a struggle to put purpose into words. This is complicated by life pressures and the lack of free time to support our psychological needs. Fortunately, cognitive psychology offers practical solutions. The use of guiding words and choices facilitates abstract conceptualization and help words flow again.

Recap

- Purpose is an essential part of health and wellbeing but may be difficult to put into words.

- Recognising that people have multiple purposes, releases us from the daunting pressure of embracing a single passion or slogan.

- Guiding words and phrases can facilitate cognitive flow and help personal purpose emerge.

Building on purpose research, theories and literature, the REVEAL tool facilitates exploration with guiding words and phrases under the following categories:

R = the RELATIONSHIPS we seek
E = the vitality and ENERGY we bring to the world
V = our VALUES
E = our path of growth and EVOLUTION
A = our ACCOMPLISHMENTS
L = our approach to LIVING TOGETHER in society

Using the REVEAL tool

When it comes to purpose exploration, one size does not fit all. For those who struggle to express life purpose, REVEAL is a hands-on, practical and playful approach. Providing a range of choices, words and phrases, REVEAL removes the barriers associated with open-ended narrative writing. If you seek to articulate your purpose, I invite you to try this self-guided approach with simple templates and instructions.

Step 1: Review the purpose words and phrases on the following pages. If these spark additional possibilities, add them in the blank spaces provided.

Step 2: Tick the checkbox next to the words and phrases that are most important to you. (You can check as many as you wish – you will narrow down your choices in the steps that follow.)

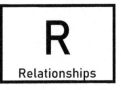

The RELATIONSHIPS we seek

- ☐ Being a good friend
- ☐ Bringing out the best in others
- ☐ Caring for animals
- ☐ Caring for family and friends
- ☐ Connecting with new people
- ☐ Helping people connect
- ☐ Mentoring/coaching/inspiring
- ☐ Providing security
- ☐ Supporting communities
- ☐ _____
- ☐ _____

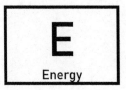

E

Energy

The vitality and ENERGY we bring to the world

- ☐ Being a calm/wise presence
- ☐ Appreciating arts/music/crafts
- ☐ Creating art/music/crafts
- ☐ Embracing an active lifestyle
- ☐ Planting and gardening
- ☐ Making people laugh
- ☐ Mobilizing change
- ☐ Proposing new ideas
- ☐ Solving problems
- ☐ _____
- ☐ _____

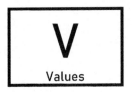

V

Values

Our VALUES

- ☐ Being accountable
- ☐ Living ethically
- ☐ Being generous
- ☐ Being grateful
- ☐ Being kind
- ☐ Leading a mindful life
- ☐ Being non-judgemental
- ☐ Being respectful
- ☐ Being spiritual
- ☐ _____
- ☐ _____

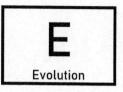

E

Evolution

Our path of growth and EVOLUTION

- ☐ Being a critical thinker
- ☐ Being curious
- ☐ Embracing new challenges
- ☐ Learning from nature
- ☐ Learning new skills
- ☐ Learning from reading/documentaries
- ☐ Learning through travel
- ☐ Navigating change
- ☐ Seeking knowledge
- ☐ _____
- ☐ _____

A
Accomplishment

Our ACCOMPLISHMENTS

- ☐ Being an entrepreneur
- ☐ Building/creating/fixing things
- ☐ Caring for clients and customers
- ☐ Helping others develop and grow
- ☐ Leading a business/organization
- ☐ Sharing my expertise/hobbies
- ☐ Taking pride in my work
- ☐ Teaching/being a scholar
- ☐ Writing/communicating
- ☐ _____
- ☐ _____

L

Living Together

Our approach to LIVING TOGETHER in society

- ☐ Addressing injustice/suffering
- ☐ Being a good listener
- ☐ Caring for nature and the environment
- ☐ Celebrating cultures
- ☐ Helping people belong
- ☐ Promoting peaceful coexisting
- ☐ Speaking up for others
- ☐ Sharing resources
- ☐ Volunteering/donating
- ☐ _____
- ☐ _____

Purpose shortlist

At this stage, you will narrow down your choices. From your REVEAL tool, copy your list of purpose words and phrases below. (Suggest no more than 10).

- _____
- _____
- _____
- _____
- _____
- _____
- _____
- _____
- _____
- _____

Pause to reflect

1. Do your purpose words and phrases lift your spirits and feel motivating?
2. Is your purpose focused on harmful or selfish intentions?
3. Is your purpose aspirational but also grounded in reality?
4. Is this *your* purpose, or is it caught up in the expectations of others?

Combine, edit, personalize

Following your refection, you will combine, edit and personalize the words and phrases from your purpose shortlist. To condense the list, you will need to prioritize. Focus on those elements you find most current and compelling (vs "someday" or "maybe").

- _____
- _____
- _____
- _____

Writing a purpose statement

As a next step, play with a few sentences bringing together key themes. Below are several examples, with special thanks to those who kindly shared their purpose statements with me:

"Sharing what I have learned in a spirit of kindness and respect. Continuously expanding my understanding of the world, learning from others and embracing new challenges."

"To take pride in my work, make beautiful things with wood and teach others. To cheer on my team in good times and bad."

"To be a helpful family-person and friend. To be nature-loving, entertaining and make people laugh."

"To be a critical thinker and problem-solver. Volunteering for causes I believe in and standing up for people in need."

"Playing music, entertaining and promoting happiness. Caring for animals and feeling grateful for the joy they bring to the world."

"Acting with generosity and kindness, seeking knowledge and connection with self, family, friends, partners and community. Developing and fostering curiosity and joy, free from judgement."

"Aspiring to empower others to identify and fulfill their life and business purpose."

"Living a mindful life, taking care of my body, spirit and mind. Being a dependable, stable and good friend, husband, father and family member. Being kind, mentoring and supportive to others."

"Being creative. Taking pride and showing professionalism in my work. Building and leading organisations and structures that work together to solve problems."

My purpose

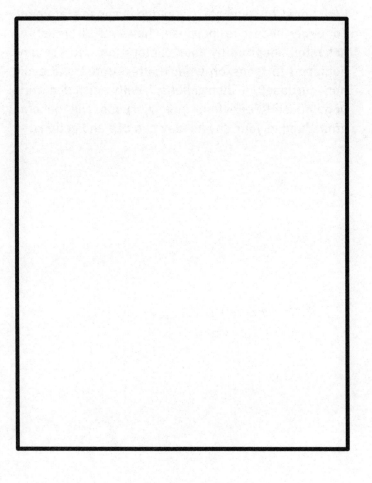

Enacting purpose

Well done! You now have a unique purpose statement. To experience life purpose, however, it must be activated. Inspired by your exploration, you are now equipped to focus on what matters most and avoid non-purposeful distractions. With practice and ongoing self-reflection, your purpose will become embedded in your day-to-day choices and actions.

Living my purpose

To live more purposefully, start with small changes. With your unique purpose in mind, what will you do more often? What will you avoid?

To live my purpose, I will do MORE of this . . .	To live my purpose, I will do LESS of this . . .

Only one hour to reveal my purpose?

Can we really find purpose in only 60 minutes? It's unlikely your exploration concluded that fast! Purpose is not permanent and continuously evolves.

Some people move quickly through the REVEAL tool while others feel one hour isn't enough. Take the time you need and revisit at different points in your life. It's hoped this book provides a tangible approach supporting a lifelong interest in purpose.

About the author

Based in Cambridge, UK (via Canada), Diane Gorsky embraced the topic of purpose at a time of personal upheaval, career change, moving continents and the global pandemic. With 20+ years of leadership and mentoring experience, an MBA and Master of Social Work degree, Diane is an international writer and speaker on the topic of purpose at the personal and organizational levels.

Connect with Diane at
reveal.purpose.book@gmail.com

Printed in Great Britain
by Amazon

36245353R00020